Captain Tim Skiba

Adventure Seeker. Ship Captain. Air Force Senior Airman. Race Car Driver. Offshore Oil Rig Captain. Auto Repair Shop Owner. "Car Guy" and Corvette Lover. Whether it is sailing his boat from Puerto Rico to Florida, competing in cross-country car racing, fighting a bull in Columbia or rescuing a downed helicopter in the Gulf of Mexico, Captain Tim has lived life to the fullest in the relentless pursuit of the next great adventure.

Captain Tim's success in business includes building a parasail company, a thriving Mortgage Company, and a successful Auto Repair Business for 18 years which by design operated without his daily involvement. With the Auto Repair business thriving on autopilot, Captain Tim steered a ship for an offshore oil rig company.

Captain Tim now shares his proven strategies to build your business to run on autopilot, giving you time and freedom to pursue your other big life goals. His life changing methods help his clients break free from limiting beliefs, shift their mindset for success and enable them to finally have the life they always dreamed of when they started their business.

Captain Tim's mission is to empower and equip you to no longer just "survive and suffer" with your pain but instead "thrive and build" the life or business to your standard the way you always wanted.

ISBN: 9798654533920

# LESS PAIN MORE GAIN

Mind Mechanic Method:

Your Trauma Survival Handbook for the Mind

Tim Skiba

# Table of Contents

# Chapter 1

# Who's Driving the Bus?

*"Your life does not get better by Chance, It gets better by Change "*

*By Jim Rohn*

Thank you for investing your time in reading this Survival Handbook. This handbook is for you. I am grateful for the opportunity to share some of my core beliefs and strategies which have served me well in good times and bad, and what has worked for my clients  as they strive to live their "best life ever!"

My goal is to share some information and techniques so you are empowered with these tools to implement in your daily life and over time, you can significantly change the way you feel and how you experience the world around you.

With the information you will be exposed to in this book you will have greater influence over your career, your health and relationships. Stop for a moment and consider. What do you want for health and wellness? What do you want to achieve in your career? What do you want to share in relationships? What are you thankful for?

We are what we think about most. What we think about tends to come to be. What we think about and focus on tends to receive our time and energy. If you are truly happy and living your dreams, congratulations, then you already have things figured out, however in challenging moments are you *thinking* or *remembering?*

Far too often we are merely remembering the past and following previous programs that seemingly match up with our present circumstances. We keep repeating the same old stories like a loop in our brain.

If you are a little bewildered in your journey, sad, angry or in any other less-than-positive state, there is some positive insight and wholesome information you can easily integrate into your life to allow you to gain a new vision, feeling the sensations, hearing words that bring you to a better place, enabling you to see the world from a whole new perspective.

To receive the most value from these techniques, here are some basic guidelines to follow as you implement and practice these skills:

A:  Allow your inner child to come out and play. Unleash your creativity.

B:  Follow your first impression, even if you feel like you're making it up.

Start with small things. The techniques will become more familiar over time, and you will build positive momentum from each step you take.

OK, are you ready?
Yes, of course you are!
The big reveal.

This is it;

If you want something, you live your life as if that thing already exists.

Go feel good.
Go feel rich.
Go feel love.
Go feel healthy.
Go feel empowered.
Go feel smart.
Go feel the sensations that bring you joy and excitement to live your best life.

Sounds easy enough, right? What's the catch? We all have our own set of rules about what must be happening to have those feelings.

The life changing solution is to reprogram ourselves to achieve them all easily and effortlessly without even thinking about it consciously.

The key was revealed to me over time as I was faced with the same problems as you might be facing today. There is no blame or regret as I share a little of my own story.

I became lost as a middle child in a family of eight. Once, my family forgot me at home on Easter Sunday because of all the confusion. My grandparents thought I was with my parents and vice versa. Fortunately, I was safe at the time and truly enjoyed the quiet.

Elementary school was OK, but I am dyslexic and reading was a big challenge throughout my twelve years of school. Still, I graduated with good grades and was truly ready for the real world.

A few weeks after graduation of highschool,I chose to join the US Air Force after looking at my options, of few local jobs and no real desire to get right back to school after graduation.  I set off to be initiated into military life. A bus ride and a plane ride across the country to San Antonio, followed by another bus ride and being herded like cattle into the military way—hurry up and wait.

As I look back, some of the tactics they used to break us down and implant their new trainees was a form of brainwashing. Most of us had been traveling all day and then we were lined up and we marched with luggage the entire time. By midnight, we all were slap happy and would do whatever we were told just to keep from getting yelled at, at least that was some of my motivation.

Some guys were already breaking down in tears. After some more training, we were shuffled to a barracks, now almost 2 a.m. to fall into our bunks and be awakened at 5 a.m. to start Day One of Basic Training.

After my chaotic family life, military discipline was a breeze. No one could get into my head like my family had. My military experience gave me even more discipline and emotional state control, being able to hold my inner thoughts to myself, no matter what the external distractions might be.

While in the USAF away from home, I received a Dear John letter from my girlfriend after only six months. I was a little lonely and went out on the town with some friends when I met the cutest young lady who let me chase her until she caught me. I was her knight in shining armor and, at the time, that worked for me. We were together for twenty challenging years and had two beautiful girls. However, there came a time when being the knight to save the day wasn't enough anymore.

What changed? And why?

After unexpectedly losing a close friend, my uncle passing from brain cancer and my business being set on fire one night, I was a little overwhelmed and at one point turned to my wife and asked for some help. This was never my style, if there was something I wanted or something that needed to be done I did it or put a plan together set forth to accomplish the task.

Our relationship of twenty years had been less than perfect and as many say we grew apart but it was not so different throughout our marriage. I learned from my father if your wife wants or needs anything a good husband does what he can to provide for his family. The thing was though I was in need and she flat out told me that was my stuff and there was nothing she could do to help. That was a big turning point in my thinking.

 If you are in the water with no help around, you must save yourself or give up and I am no quitter. I didn't quit, I took a deep breath and stuck to it and started to focus on myself. I started to ask myself better questions, not why but how.  How can I do better? How can I work things out? I shifted my focus and mindset, bringing back all my life lessons, to find the best of them and letting go of what didn't work, keeping the gold.

We did part ways. I found myself in a new situation, still rebuilding myself and the business that had burned. A new relationship entered my life and so did a number of other challenges.

I was challenged in all aspects of life during the upcoming years, relationships, finances and health.

Relationships and money are things that if we choose to, we can make a plan, do the work and make changes for the better.

Health or illness is a little different because it moves so subtly through our life at times we don't pay it much attention until we get that scary report you have three options and no guarantee except no one gets out alive.

The final key that really confirmed all I had learned was when the love of my life was diagnosed with a rare terminal disease. This was a turning point for me. This was something I could not control or fix. It was not my body.

I had been trained in diagnostics for years but not in the field of medicine and for a short period of time I simply stepped back and supported her in her decisions. I was passive on her healthcare choices.

In an effort to steady myself, I did what I always did and that was to ask questions so I started my own journey of understanding how other people could and did get healing and life changing events when they changed what they believed.

I will say now and in all my works, that people will get what they truly believe. I learned the real change has to happen at the core level, *your deepest fears and your inner identity.*

You are lucky to be reading this now because you have more power to create massive change than you have ever thought. You have the power to create miracles in your life because I have seen it in so many others.

My wife's change came in many ways but she is here today because of the shift in her beliefs and mindset. It happened one day sitting on the couch, as I was guiding her through a meditation that she finally let go of the fears that had been tormenting her for most of her life. I am happy to say that she is still with me and that she has far exceeded any beliefs that her doctors had for her. She is in remission and we are now "living" our new life.

I believe we have more influence on our health, relationships and careers than I did only a few years ago. The skills shared here are to help you take some of the randomness out of your everyday life.

Simply continue on your journey of discovery of the expanding possibilities that lay before you.

# Chapter 2

# **WHAT!**

What..What...WHAT _______________!

*If we wait until we're ready, we will be waiting for the
rest of our life.*

*Unknown*

I have focused on the general, because resolution
of your challenges is my goal to help you in your
journey to live your best life.  So the real question
is, why do I even need these tools and techniques?
Because unless you have been raised by enlightened
individuals or have studied brain science, quantum
physics and alternative healing practices, you probably have not yet been exposed or experienced the
power of these simple techniques.

# Trauma

Trauma, be it physical or mental is the culprit, the experience of putting your system into shock, an altered state. Your body reacts to each of these situations in different ways because it is designed to do so to keep you safe and alive.

Trauma to the body is usually evident, unless it is internal, and even then there are usually signs a problem exists. With physical trauma there is shock to the natural flow of your system. When the body is traumatized, there are automatic physical reactions. Fluids and blood are immediately pumped to the injured location. Depending on the severity of the trauma, the body might even go into shock. This is to help you understand when the normal system is interrupted by a trauma, our pre-programmed response is a good thing.

With the mind we are designed with similar systems and responses but there are little to no visible signs for others to know what we have experienced. Therefore most of us go through our lives striving to figure out what it all means and how to work through our "stuff". The funny thing is that each person is different in their response or reaction to a trauma, one person  might have no emotional impact while another might be overwhelmed.

For example driving fast is a relative term. Most people on the highway would think fast is 55 mph to 70 mph. When you start driving you build up to higher and higher speeds tolerance. Would going 100 mph be traumatic or scary for someone? Maybe.  What about 200 plus mph? For most race car drivers that is merely a Sunday drive. This is an example of the extreme and to be in a car that is going 200 mph could be traumatizing because of the unusual experience of moving more than twice as fast as usual, but put the same person in a plane and 200 mph is slow. Once again speed is a relative experience depending on the situation. Most people can relate to speed and it is a measurable experience.

As for the emotional experience, that comes down to each and every individual person's perspective. This is why emotional trauma is so difficult to measure, see, understand or identify.

What one person says was terrifying, the next might have felt exhilarated or nothing at all. The feelings that someone feels are real for them and for whatever reason, if it is working for them, great. If it is not working for them, then there is good news.

The information and techniques I am sharing here are some ways for you to be more empowered to have more control over some of the less than positive triggers in your life. Some of my best clients have shared with me that although these techniques appear to be simple, they are highly effective and very powerful,  saving them time and money over the other methods they tried.

**Case study: Go or no go**

Dan was a chief engineer on a cargo plane and during a special ops flight over the ocean, there was a shift in the cargo and things became critically dangerous very quickly. There was a clear and present danger for the crew and the plane. Dan instinctively did everything he was trained to do in this situation saving the day. However, after the plane safely landed, he had no recall of what had happened, what he had done or how much time had passed. Only when the other crew members called to him did his sense of time and place come back to his awareness.

Over the next year he was awarded for saving the flight and crew but he was not able to recall the lapse in time nor was he able to get back on the plane to do his job. He went through weeks of counseling to recall the event and eventually did but without resolve of the emotional issues. After hearing his story I asked what he was feeling and he replied he didn't feel like he had done anything special and was not deserving of all the attention he received.   Even after all the counselling to bring the memory back, he had no idea why he had blocked out that time in the first place.

The mind is designed to do this.  In extreme situations our mind is designed to protect us.  If we survive the event it saves the information so we don't repeat it. This can be a good thing but when it stops us from moving forward it can disrupt our lives.

For Dan, we identified a link associated with an event in his childhood. He never gave a thought that a childhood trauma could affect his job, however as an adult it blocked the events to protect him on the plane. Only after linking the two events did he realise he actually acted as the hero, deserving all the awards and recognition he received.

The trauma of the plane was not the original problem, the underlying problem had been hiding in the background, only disrupting his life subtly until he was faced with a life or death situation and he did the right thing.

This example is just the tip of the iceberg of how a small event in our childhood can linger and influence our adult life. Trauma doesn't have to be a huge event from anyone else's perspective but when you're in a heightened emotional state, be it a happy state, angry state or fearful state and something is anchored to it, chances are you will recall similar feelings later in life.  Similar to when you hear your favorite song or you smell home cooking from your childhood and you are instantly transported back to that time and the feeling linked to it.

Trauma is an event that disrupts the system. The information I am sharing with you are the  tools and techniques to help you work through your personal traumas, returning to an unencumbered being, ready to take on the world!

# Case Study: Compassion Enables Freedom

David was a very successful manager of a construction company that did work all around the world for the military. He had wanted to join the military and be part of one of the elite forces but because of his experience with the law he was not eligible. However, his dream of being an elite risk taker never stopped as he had an opportunity to go to work with a contractor who built very large tents for special operations for our military. The risky, dangerous part was working over a 100 feet in the air. David was drawn right in--the risk, the adventure and working side-by-side with special forces guys around the world.

Things seemed to be going great, money had allowed him to buy a million dollar home in Vegas and he had two children and a beautiful wife. The challenge was that he was missing out on a life with his own family and his son was acting out at home, angry all the time and he was at a loss.

He loved his family and was providing a good life for them, but his drive and focus was always on his work. He was truly torn.

David shared his story with me of how he was raised by his prostitute mother until the age of 5 when he was forced into a situation to defend himself and he stabbed her in the hand.  Shortly after that she was sent to jail for neglect. He then stayed with his father and father's boyfriend.  At a very young age he was exposed to drugs, alcohol and murders.  He learned how to use a gun at a very young age and had to use one when he was 13 to defend his brother who was being attacked.

Because of the survival techniques he developed as a child and had to use growing up, he felt his son needed to be tough and would tell him that he was the man of the house at age 4 and was supposed to take care of his mother and sister while he was gone.

His son was being raised in a totally different environment than he had been but being put in the position of man of the house was a big responsibility and was showing in the son's behavior.

After using a couple of visualization techniques to re-solve his emotional baggage,  he discovered that his early traumatic experiences had shown up as a poor self image and he was staying away from home to pro-tect his family.  His worthiness to have a loving, caring family was discovered.

David was instantly able to have compassion for his younger self, freeing him to be the kind of husband and father he had dreamed he could be.

Have you ever wondered how our thoughts happen or what we are made of? There are a few deep thinkers who spend most of their time working to understand these questions. They are physicists. They have many theories about what the smallest particles of matter con-sist of, and they have many different names for those particles. Over time, they have been able to do more and more tests due to new technology.

These scientists discovered very small particles would sometimes act like a solid particle and other times they would act like a wave. Today we understand everything is ultimately made up of energy. Most people have heard about protons, neutrons and electrons, but there are even smaller particles with an electrical signal or signature.

Eventually, after many years of research, experiments and study, they determined the thoughts of the observer actually affected the test results.

How does that relate to us?

Have you ever been near someone and without any visible interaction, gotten a positive feeling by being in their presence? What is that energy?

On the other hand, have you felt an uneasiness while in the presence of a total stranger? Where do those feelings come from?

These uneasy feelings come through energy which you are receiving via your heart.

These sensations can be measured with high-tech and not-so-high-tech measuring devices I would simply call them feeling. Most of us have experienced that gut feeling. More times than not, it served us well. The times we chose not to follow our internal guidance system " feelings", we usually ended up repeating a lesson that can be more painful the second or third time around before we learn the lesson.

Have you ever had a feeling where you simply knew something good was going to happen?

How about a thought something not so good was about to happen?

Do you believe your thoughts had any impact on the outcome? We are constantly sending and receiving information on many levels including the quantum level, possibly more so than any of us want to believe.

Why do new winners seem to win more after they won the first time? Possibly they are totally convinced they can do it again because it has already happened.

Let's suppose they already believed it before it happened?

Imagine that many of the people watching the competition believed that it was the right time for a new outcome?

What if their opponents believed it might happen, too, because they were intimidated or felt they were personally off their game?

We live in a world of infinite possibilities. These examples only scratch the surface of what the deep thinkers spend lifetimes trying to figure out. My *personal* goal is to improve the odds for obtaining my desires and decrease some of the randomness in my life, so I can live in a more peaceful state. My *desire is* to give you some tools to do the same.

Throughout my life, with every challenge, I learned and I changed. I grew in many ways, which is what I am sharing in this book. These lessons and survival techniques can be used by anyone to improve their journey.

The bottom line: some basic drivers guide our decisions. If we don't understand them, they will haphazardly lead us by default. These drivers make up the subconscious mind and that's our next topic of discussion.

In Chapters to follow we are going to explore four profound  techniques, *"Formula One Restart, Loony Cartoon Reframe, Framing Technique* and finally, *Spinning Technique.*

After experiencing these techniques, you will instantly:

A. feel better about your past experiences

B. feel empowered when confronted by challenging relationships

C. learn to dissolve and resolve some of the negative emotions connected to your difficult memories

What I'm hoping you will receive by completing these chapters, is a new perspective on life and happiness, along with some powerful tools to experience your life anew.

There are three things to accelerate each process:

- Play along, believing your inner child.
- Follow your first impression while practicing with each technique.
- Start small, allowing the process to become more familiar.

Journaling opportunity

- Write down a little about the good times in your story.
- Recall a time you were influenced by being in or around a person or group.
- Write out things you *believe* will happen and somethings you *hope* will happen.

### *Call To Peace**

*When all is simply wonderful, find  a place on your person to place a trigger point.  Now easily, in an instant, you can recall all the good feelings you are internally experiencing.  Practice this instinctively,  easily recovering your positive attitude,  recovering it easier each time again and again, helping you to continuously improve your performance, just as an athlete performs that perfect routine while in a perfect state of openness. Make being at peace within and around you the familiar.*

*Tim Skiba*

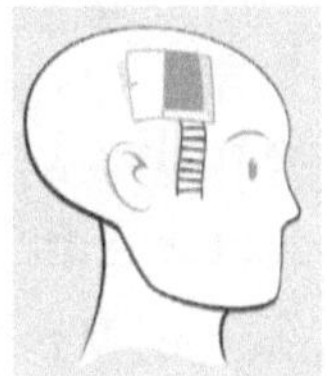

# Chapter 3

# Your Subconscious and Preparing for Change

*Your subconscious mind is 30,000 times more power-ful than your conscious mind.*

*By T. Robbins*

The role of the subconscious mind is to simply keep us safe. If we are in a risky situation, and we do something that works, our subconscious will automate the process and deliver the same response each time it is faced with similar circumstances.

If we keep looking at the past and questioning what we could have done differently, we are missing out on what is right in front of us, right here and right now. What we "should have done" is now in the past. The present is what we have power over now. Now is where we can make changes.

We, as humans, have to realize that we do not have the power to destroy or create matter. We do, however, have the power to change it. We are exactly where we should be to experience something our soul wants to experience. Once we understand experiences are nei-ther good nor bad, we can  appreciate that they are merely lessons. That's when we can see the good in all situations as events guiding us to our next experience.

State of Being Safe

Think about all the events of this year. Some memories are uplifting or light and some may not be so colorful.  I invite you to stop for a moment and notice one memory which catches your attention. Now focus on this one moment in time and this one memory.

Where are you at this moment? Inside or outside? Sitting or standing? A quiet place or a loud one? Dressed or undressed?  What are you wearing? What do you smell?  What do you hear?  Are you safe or not safe in this memory?

Right now as you recall that memory, are you relative-
ly safe? How many times throughout this last year did
you feel safe? I have had some clients reveal to me that
they hardly ever feel safe and that is why I am sharing
some secrets to help you work toward a safer feeling.

In general, we take note of the extremes like the weath-
er, those dog days of summer and the snow day that
shut everything down. I have worked on the water as
a ship captain for several years, and for the most part,
the days are generally calm and uneventful, yet over
the years I've also been in seas with 18-foot waves and
sometimes been very ill. On several occasions I partici-
pated in life saving rescues.

Acknowledging to yourself that most of the time you
are safe and truly receiving that, frees you from un-
needed stress. You can be in the moment achieving
your goals and accomplish the tasks at hand. Safe is
a feeling interpreted by our senses when a set of our
own rules are met. **If you are not feeling safe, then
fear is in charge and your entire body is reacting
to that fear.** My goal is to empower you with some
of these tools to simply allow you to feel safer. When
you are free of fear, you are truly open to look for the
gold. Look for the good at all times so you can simply
continue to live your dreams.

## Testimonial:  Lana

"I've been doing sessions with Capt. Tim Skiba for a couple of years now and he has helped me so much. One incident stands out in my mind. It was a Thanksgiving dinner that went terribly wrong. It was my first family gathering after my divorce and I was so excited to see everyone.  However, things happened and I ended up sobbing after everyone left.

In my next session, Tim helped me to see that this emotional storm had its source in past trauma and pain. We dissolved the past pain quickly and easily. I immediately felt free and clear. What a relief.

I've been to several family gatherings since then and no more emotional incidents. When things happen, I just take a breath and let the moment pass right over me. I'm so happy because I can still attend these events and be with my family without fear of getting triggered."

## Entrainment

Fortunately, our perspective can be changed in strategic ways. The process of changing through synchronizing with an outside influence is called *entrainment.* This phenomenon occurs all the time at many levels, including at a quantum level.

A good example of entrainment or mirroring is when we fall into alignment with a dominant or consistent force, even if it is not our own species. This is why animals can be so therapeutic for people in stressful states. An agitated human will sync up with the calmness of a service animal after only a few minutes.

We all are continuously looking for a match. As you go through your day, be the person you truly want to find...someone caring, helpful, pleasant, hardworking, calm, compassionate, loving or any other features you're looking for, whether you're seeking a friend, life partner, or a mentor.

The following information and techniques are designed to give you the tools to take some of the randomness out of your life, and enable you to have more influence over yourself and others.

## FORMULA ONE RESTART

The Formula One Restart is designed to clean up and release the bad feelings you have about random and not so random things in your world.

The journey only takes a few minutes and can be extremely helpful to free you from some of the clutter that gets in the way of getting what we intuitively want... to be happy.

Reading through the Formula One Restart process will help you become more familiar with the journey. The more playful and animated you are, the more effective the process is, so really get into it, be creative and let your body and mind take action in a very energetic way. Simply have fun with it. There is no right or wrong. You are the driver in this Formula One Racecar and always have been. There are always signs and general guidelines but the real change is directed by you.

The Formula one restart process is a technique that is used to clear away some less than positive feelings that can be holding you back. It takes about 20 minutes to go through this guided journey using non specific metaphors allowing you to release the emotionally charged feelings while not having to share anything specific, easily clearing your mind to move forward. Using your creative mind skills and engaging your physical body with simple movements of looking around and reaching out, connecting the mind body experience.. This process can be used daily and is designed to help open you to the great possibilities that are available, as you learn more about how to get the most out of your truly powerful mind.

We are simply working with feelings and sensations and the way we interpret information from our senses. You will become more familiar with the sensations and patterns of your body and mind and how there is a totally natural feedback loop. As you start to focus on more positive emotions, you will intuitively realize how good things can happen, even out of the less than positive situations.

   –   Meditation for Formula One Restart

**Audio Recording available at:**
**https://youtu.be/i4nVZOecktU**


*Warning: This is a meditative process and you should be in a safe place without interruption and not be driving or operating any forms of equipment. It is recommended that you refer to the audio version and use headphones for best results.*

As we start, find a quiet place where you can go through this process. You may sit in a comfortable chair to relax to the fullest, or lie down in a comfortable safe space. As you prepare yourself, your mind and body, have your legs straight and arms down towards your sides or gently lying on your lap.

Starting to become aware of your body with each breath you take, simply taking the clean air into your lungs. You may yawn, stretch your arms or neck muscles, starting to signal the rest of your body it is totally fine to continue to relax, with each breath you take, and now might be a good time to close your eyes because as your eyes close, you can become even more at ease. Now focusing on your breathing, taking in a large breath and holding it a little longer than normal, holding, holding, slowly, intentionally counting down, Five, now to Four, deeper to Three, Two all the way down to One.

Noticing as your breathing slows, your mind begins to clear, releasing again breathing in a deep breath now, again holding, simply counting it all down Five holding Four easily to Three deeper Two all the way releasing with One.

Now, with each relaxing breath you can go deeper, allowing your focus to move to areas around your body, the space that surrounds you, and thinking about how your body occupies the space, now focusing on your body in the space, noticing your feet, the sensation of your feet relaxing in this space, with each thought you can easily release any tension in your body, allowing things to be just as easily released in your mind, as we continue on this journey.

Noticing positive sensations moving up from your feet to your legs, continuously allowing the relaxing breath to flow through every cell of your body, feeling the sensations easily move to your abdomen, noticing the sensations of your abdomen in space slowly moving sensations upward towards your stomach to acknowledge to your body all is well.

Relaxing, deeper sensations moving toward the chest, heart and lungs completely cleansing with each breath flowing through in and around your body, now easily moving into the shoulders, flowing through the arms, all the way down to the hands and pushing any leftover stress out through the fingertips.

As you notice the body has released, the positive healing sensations rise from the shoulders into the neck and completely easily into the head, filling the entire body and mind with your positive healing sensations allowing you to focus on a safe place, your safe place.

This safe place could be a totally real place you remember as a child or the dream place that simply brings you peace, or possibly it could be an imaginary fantasy place that is truly perfect in every way. As you focus on your place, a place you feel safe, you may have even more powerful sensations easily flowing through your body and mind noticing the sensations, feeling the change as you are empowered at the speed of thought.

Now within this safe place, you are able to experience true positive changes in your mind and body to your standards. Now focusing on a point in front of you, possibly a little light that you can barely make out. Using your power to bring it into focus, it appears to be shining metal and as it becomes clearer, it is a door. As you approach the door, you notice it is locked.  You see a keypad to the side. This pad is for you, and as you focus on the pad, the numbers to release the combination are revealed to you and you are now easily able to open the door. As you open the door, you are pleasantly greeted by a warm glowing light. Now, as you enter this place, the warm glowing light is a small fire and you are easily able to move closer, and as you do, you notice you are in this warm feeling place with a dome shape, like the inside of an egg.

As you look around, you can see more clearly on the walls, that there are papers and these papers represent all the positive sensations you feel, all the positive emotions and events in your life. These are glowing in a certain color now. As you look even closer, you start to see some have a different color, a distinct difference in color, as it becomes clearer these represent your less than positive emotions and events, things that may have held you back and now you are truly ready to let them go, now you can easily instinctively reach out and grasp one of those less than positive colors.  You are easily able to crush it up and now you simply throw it into the fire.

As it enters the fire there is a rush of heat and the sound of crackling as the releasing energy empowers you, notice the change, feeling the heat from the fire, seeing the flames grow back in the sensations, not yet but in a moment, you can easily repeat the action and continue to receive positive energy.

Now simply find another, once again reaching out for one of those less than positive colors pulling one off the wall, again crumpling it up, now throwing it into the fire, noticing the change, noticing the positive changes filling your body, and the room.

Now once again you are able to reach out to remove one of those less than positive colors from your special place, and then take it in your hands, smashing it easily, now throwing it into the fire, creating an even larger blaze.

Now how easy is this for you? You are able to use whatever method you desire to scan the room for all the remaining less than positive colors, sometimes others use an aid like an x-ray or a search light to find each and every less than positive paper because some like to hide, and you are empowered to find them all. As you search, you are able to process them at the speed of thought, crushing or crumpling them up, as fast or as slowly as you like, and throwing  them into the fire, creating a grand blaze.

Take whatever time you need, and as you do, notice the change as you are able to easily release the block that may have held you back, or might have tainted something good.

Now you are truly cleansed, being freed from any less than positive feelings. As you scan the room for any stragglers that might be hiding, feel the positive warmth. And as you scan the room, you notice that every place you removed something negative, that the totally positive color has now filled in, creating a wonderful feeling, totally surrounding you, filling your body mind and soul with good feelings, using all your senses to intuitively recognize all the good, all the benefits, all the truly wonderful positive effects of releasing and freeing yourself can be.

Simply soak it all in to your standards, giving you a new perspective and a new power. With this new power, you are empowered with more energy to accomplish your goals and this new power will just as easily allow you to rest deeper.

Not now but in a moment, we will be leaving this place, carrying all the benefits you have received and at any time you choose, you are able to return and simply recreate your experience to your standards, remembering all you need and let the rest go.

Now we will count up from one to five, coming back to this place we call reality.

Starting with One receiving all the positive benefits of this journey, this was all for you. You took the time, you made the choice and you have received the rewards.

Two, remembering all you learned for your betterment empowering you to live your best life.

Three, for every situation, challenge or event there are always three solutions, three choices, three answers and now they will come to you easily intuitively from this moment forward.

Four, yes, it is all for you, you did the work you made the journey, you took the time you received the benefits.

And now Five coming back to this world we call reality, only at the speed you feel comfortable, and when you are ready, you can open your eyes. Simply, take whatever time you need to refocus on the here and now, feeling rested, refreshed and totally aware.

**REFLECTION:**

1. Make a short list of time and places you feel safe and another when and where you are not so safe.
2. After reading or experiencing the Formula One Restart how do you feel different or what would you like to feel different about?
3. Bask in the freedom of taking control of your life lessons, allowing each and every one of them to guide you to your best life.

## Positive Changes

*As you move through your day and life, the truly won-
derful, positive changes will simply get easier.
Things will continuously get better every day in every way.
With each breath that you take and every beat of
your heart, it is you, simply trading up to the ideals
of your best life.*

*Tim Skiba*

# Process Your Fears

*"He who has overcome his fears will truly be free."*
*By Aristotle*

When we humans were alone in the wilderness—and it was all wilderness—**our natural instincts  kept us alive.**

Let's use a giant saber-toothed tiger as an example, simply because I like tigers. Suppose it's 10,000 years in the past and you are alone in the forest foraging for the little berries the birds are eating. All is calm. The sun is warming your back. The birds are singing their songs and your heart is filled with love, thinking of how happy your family will be to receive these berries.

Then the sound of a snapping twig changes everything. This simple sound triggers your body and suddenly you feel different. Adrenaline floods your system. Your senses are instantly in overdrive: scanning the bushes, listening for more sounds, muscles tensed to fight, flight or freeze, so you can survive whatever may happen in the next few minutes.

The moment you get a glimpse of the giant saber tooth tiger slinking through the woods, you're no longer thinking. You're in automatic mode, operating from your subconscious mind that has kept you alive up to this point. Your fear response is at the deepest core of your survival system.

What happens next? Do you run? Climb a tree? Stand still and wait for the tiger to pass?

Which tactic will work? Which tactic worked before? At this point in our imaginary story, what would you do?

If you had survived a tiger before now, you will probably use the same tactics again. If those tactics work again today, **this behavior will become part of your automated programming system in your subconscious mind.**

This imaginary prehistoric you is not so different from you today.

That person had behaviors based on love (gathering berries for the family) and fear (running from a tiger). And so do you.


## LOVE OR FEAR

Love can be simply described by positive emotions: peaceful, safe, joyful, happy, compassionate, triumphant, thrilled and the list goes on.

Fear also comes with many names, almost twice as many as those associated with love, including anger, frustration, hatred, loss of any kind, upset, mad, depressed and more.

Is this too simple a concept to say we are either in a state of love or in a state of fear? It is a black and white contrast with little gray. The gray is in how far we cross the line and how long we choose to linger away from love.

If love were light, as a word describing goodness, fear is something we creep into like walking into a forest on a dark night. The darker it gets, the more lost we feel, until eventually we might not make it back to our safe place.

Stories of the dark instill fear in us—in movies, books, and around the campfire at night. The uncertainty of what might be lurking in the dark brings up our animal instincts for survival.

In modern times, fear can be triggered by a coworker, an in-law, the boss or simply embarrassment because we didn't know something. Road rage has the same fight-or-flight reaction over thirty feet of highway, only now we have a 3,000-pound car to use as a weapon or for protection.

You are not so different from your prehistoric self from long ago. You might have replayed the tiger story in your head, but you still have to go out foraging to stay alive. What does this truly mean to you right now?

Although today's dangers are different than back then, many dangers are still out there. In the old days, a person might have one or two life-threatening events a month. In our world today, we could be looking the Grim Reaper in the eye every time we drive to work.

Many of us feel that surge of adrenaline every time the boss walks into our office, or simply receiving a text from the person you don't want to hear from, who just won't stop. Can you relate to any of these emotional events?

These all trigger the same fear response in you as a saber-toothed tiger would have triggered the early man.

You'll have all the same internal physical reactions: a surge in norepinephrine to trigger your fight or flight response to stress and adrenaline to scale back your immune system, at the same time reducing the feel-good chemicals dopamine and oxytocin. Although your system might be working properly now, however being triggered continuously will more than likely cause long-term consequences.

**The subconscious mind will continue to automate your responses that worked before, even when they are no longer in your best interest.**

The only way to change this is to upload new, upgraded programming. More about that soon.

## MY OWN FEAR STORY

My own story of fear was one concerning my own family, however  I didn't realize how the trauma had impacted my life for so many years.

When I became aware of it, I reframed it by taking away the fear and loneliness and filling the void with the loving, caring story I'd always deserved.

**I uploaded new programming, and you can, too.**

Oddly enough, my fear was being around people whom I knew. In fact, strangers never bothered me.

My mother told me stories for years of how I would hide in the closet when I was only two years old. She would look all around the house calling my name. I would be so quiet, once I was in a full-size wingback chair inches from her and she couldn't find me.

She would laugh at how cute I was. When she finally found me, she would ask, "What are you doing there hiding?"

I was the fourth of four children in her first four years of marriage. She was an only child and always wanted to have a big family. She got her wish and eventually had two more children a few years later. To say the least, she was not prepared and became quite overwhelmed in a small house full of kids.  My mother withdrew to the point that we were largely unsupervised and my older siblings often got rough with each other.

I was the littlest kid for a long time. Not able to have the upper hand. My self-preservation technique was to find a low-traffic location and stay quiet. This tactic worked for me and became part of my automated programming.

As I grew older, I became even more withdrawn and shy.  I struggled in school with Dyslexia. After starting college, I learned about my learning disorder, although by that time they said I had adapted and there was really nothing to do differently.

The adaptive process was another tactic that served me well. I learned to reduce things down to a consumable size and to check my work multiple times to safeguard against further embarrassment.

**We all adapt to survive.**

Some tactics can be beneficial to living our best lives, but others are less productive and produce undesirable side effects.

The thing is, we don't know what we don't know. Which ones are beneficial and which are not? This is exactly why I am sharing my discoveries with you here.

Fear is a built-in safety mechanism designed to help keep you safe, but anything overused can lose its effectiveness or can overpower the internal conversation and get in the way.

Case Study:  Rediscovering Her Voice

Dawn is a paralegal for a large legal group. She left New York to live her dreams in California because it was as far away from New York as she could imagine at the time, however she only had enough money to make it to Arizona. She found a job and was doing well working with people one-on-one over the phone.

The conflict arose whenever she was forced into a group situation. She would shut down and withdraw to a quiet corner trying not to be noticed.  These tactics were holding her back from moving up in her career. Working with her over the phone we discovered when she was only 6 years old her mother had some friends over and she was scolded for playing so loudly. Dawn could see and remember every person in the room and even the toys she was playing with and how they all looked at her, instantly changing her entire program-ming with one emotional event.

Her mother never knew what had happened that day but when she told Dawn to be quiet when people come around that is exactly what she did, because Dawn simply wanted to please her mother. From that point forward Dawn would just be quiet when others were around. Dawn even asked herself, "Why is no one else quiet?" She also thought, "Why only me?" and "Why doesn't my mother know why I am being so quiet?" Dawn was angry and frustrated for twenty five years.  After a short period working with me, *she found her voice and the joy to freely accomplish great things.*

**REFLECTION**

1. Can you recall a time in your life when you lived in a state of love and peace? What did or does that look and feel like?

2. Can you recall a time in your life when you suffered a trauma that caused you fear and took your peaceful state of mind away?

3. What was your survival technique?

**REBIRTH**

*New day, like any other day, we have a routine we follow that has become a habit. As you start with the steps of your day simply intentionally start to become aware of what you are doing that instantly brings joy to you.*

*What brings up those warm feelings?*

*Consciously breathe deeply as you focus on those wonderful thoughts, continuously linking the positive emotions to the relaxation of deep breathing, now stepping forward to your next stage of your daily routine.*

*Once again allowing a joyful thought, hold your awareness while simultaneously following your steps that help you reach your goals continuously, linking your relaxing deep intake of life- giving oxygen, naturally filling your body. At times subconsciously trying to go back to an old less than positive state. Now knowing you are empowered by your knowledge of your past, you can easily shift your joyful thoughts to your focus again and then again, shifting your joyful thoughts to your focus allowing you to live life in a new way, intuitively stronger by the speed of thought enlightened to the forces of grace, sending you the signals to warn you properly of challenges that are ahead. You can instantly notice the difference, now totally engaged in truly joyful thoughts as the world moves you amazingly move forward with a new found grace,  an awesome awareness of living life to a standard you totally approve of from now on, in all situations you have new insight to live your best life. This is your rebirth to the life of your dreams.*

*Love, joy and peace in and around you always!*

*Tim Skiba*

# The Nature of Safety

*Judging a person does not define who they are ...*
*it defines who you are.*

*Unknown*

## SAFETY/JUDGMENT

Do you hate being judged? I certainly do. How I judge myself is even worse than the misinformed judgment by others. They'll never know how hard I have worked to get that job, raise, new house, a new car, etc., upon which they are judging me. From childhood we are instructed by our parents not to pass judgment on other people, however, making judgment calls is necessary because we all have a primal need to make judgments to keep ourselves safe.

Judging self and judging situational safety are connected through the judging process but the side effects are the emotional feelings that are linked to the judgements and how we store and process them. Our modern world requires us to judge whether to engage our fight-or-flight response five, ten, twenty or more times a day. If there is no real emotional connection, a simple judgment call might take a few seconds or less, no harm no foul. However, for important judgment calls, we ponder and may not know the outcome for a long time.

Take a moment and think. Are you dealing with a judgment call right now?  Can you feel that knot in your neck or shoulder or stomach? Everyone has felt this same feeling at one time or another.

Is your decision really life or death? If yes, give it time and focus on it. An important decision deserves the time to make that call. Do the work. Measure twice and cut once, as they say.

On the other hand, if this decision is not important, step back a bit. Push it away from being right in your face. Once again, carefully measure twice and make the judgment.

How do you deal with the aftermath? The simple answer:

**make a decision to the best of your ability, then intuitively move on and put it behind you.**

That being said, can you do that? Or are you carrying all those past judgments with you? If you've let them all go, then great. You're on your way.

If, however, you are still carrying the burden of shame or judgment I encourage your continued learning and when you feel the need for more, simply reach out to me and I will be open to helping you navigate to a better place.

www.mindmechanicmethod.com


**EMOTIONAL SAFETY:**

Have you ever had someone say something that wasn't nice and this person had no real idea what happened? The words cut right through everything and stuck in your heart. Now you have a picture and a face and sounds and emotions.

Will this story help you the rest of the day, week or month or will it just hurt? There is always a lesson to learn and that is good, that is what we want to keep and let the negative emotions go.

There's a simple and easy way to release yourself from the past. You can have control over it now.  If it's not a positive in your life, you'll feel so much better if you just let it go. That leads you to a powerful tool that can instantly release the emotional charge left from a less than desirable event and free you from the long-term side effects.

Let's go over it and it will likely be common sense for you, and reviewing it a couple of times will surely increase its effectiveness.

## *Framing Technique*

The Framing technique is a very useful tool, instantly changing your state. Once again using your creative mind and body to manipulate an event either in your past of many years or merely moments ago.

You are easily able to keep the lessons and let the rest go. This technique can be used at will in a matter of seconds freeing you instantly from an emotional charged memory.

### *Meditation for Framing Technique*

Video available at: https://youtu.be/9Eeg5scavws

*Warning:  This is a meditative process and you should be in a safe place without interruption and not be driving or operating any forms of equipment. It is recommended that you refer to the audio version and use headphones for best results.*

This is an easy technique you can use instantly to free yourself of old emotions.  Initially you may want to find a place that is comfortable and quiet but as you become more familiar with the technique you will be able to do it at any time, anywhere. Take a deep, slow cleansing breath, clearing your mind and relaxing your body. Now the healing begins…

First start by imagining that less than positive thought or event that is preoccupying your life and feel the emotion tied to it.

Locate the feeling in or around you. It could be in your head, your heart, your gut, or some other place. Yes, it has to be there or it wouldn't be bothering you.

Imagine that feeling is like a ball of energy. Just pretend and play along for a moment. Pull out that ball of energy and build a pile of that energy in your hand.

Stretch the ball out like a TV and draw a big black frame around it. This is to isolate the event and focus on it.

Now, focus on the image associated with the feeling, is it a video playing in front of you or a picture. Is it in color or black and white?

Remember the Old TV sets that had a knob to adjust for contrast. Imagine that knob on the bottom of your frame. Simply turn the knob so the image either blacks out or whites out, whichever feels better.

When you know it's blanked out, take your writing hand and imagine you have a magic gold marker on the tip of your writing finger. Take whatever time you need and write inside the blank frame what's important about this event. This process is so easy because you don't have to know what you are writing. Your subconscious mind always knows, and that's enough. Just write until you feel complete.

When you're finished writing, hold the frame by the sides and shrink it down to the size of a postage stamp.

Raise it up over your head and effortlessly throw it behind you, all the way back. Instantly you feel a change.

Now, your index finger turns into an imaginary nail gun. Point the nail gun back over your shoulder and nail that frame in the past, intuitively, instinctively completely putting it in the past where it belongs. The information is available if needed but, like your old taxes on a shelf somewhere, totally forgotten.

If you want to test to see if you can bring back the feeling, that's ok, but in most cases, it is truly best left in the past.

Use this simple technique over and over again to instantly shed yourself of limiting beliefs and free yourself from feelings that hold you back from being your best you. Start with small things and as you become more familiar with the technique you can effortlessly use it to instinctively make the choices and changes that meet your standards and expectations.

**Most of us shower or clean our bodies daily. Simply cleansing your mind and memories of unworthy thoughts is just as important, so you can start fresh and live your dreams.**


## REFLECTION

1. List judgment calls you have had to make on a regular basis.
2. What are some decisions that you are still waiting to make?
3. Make a list of memories you would like to easily put in the past where they belong.


### *Quiet place*

*You visit me here without space and time*
*Far from the noise we all find*
*It's simply a quiet place in my mind*


*Tim Skiba*

# Chapter 6

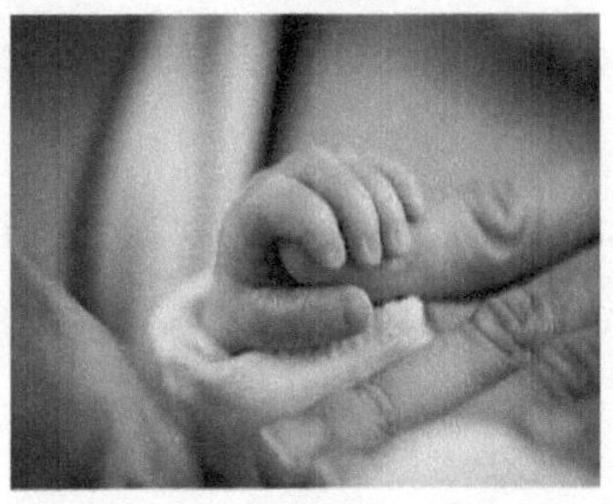

# Love or Fear?

*When you choose to perceive love over fear, Life be-
gins to flow.*

*By Gabrielle Berstein*

How we process any sensory input comes from our first experiences, perhaps even before we were born. Whether the input was good, bad or otherwise, doesn't matter. Some feeling that originally brought comfort might be stored as good or pleasurable, a physical response or maybe a smile. This smile could have influenced our early caregiver to repeat that experience and reinforce it with another smile. If a baby smiles at you while playing peek-a-boo, then you are more likely to play the game over and over, creating a pleasurable moment for both parties.  The same happens on the discomfort side. Unfortunately crying doesn't produce a smile response. This communication skill can be limited.

**Even now, I still have to stop at times to focus on the sensations and figure out what the input I am feeling really means.**

### A Train of Pain

*I hurt*
*I feel a sensation of discomfort*
*I have a sense of uncertainty*
*I feel helpless*
*I long for a light to shine in the darkness*
*But none is for myself*
*It is for a love of my life*
*These sensations are a reflection of my own past*
*When I could not see the light*
*When I was helpless*
*When pain was a way of life*

*Tim Skiba*

Sensory input is merely information, like the sound of a siren. Information gives guidance.

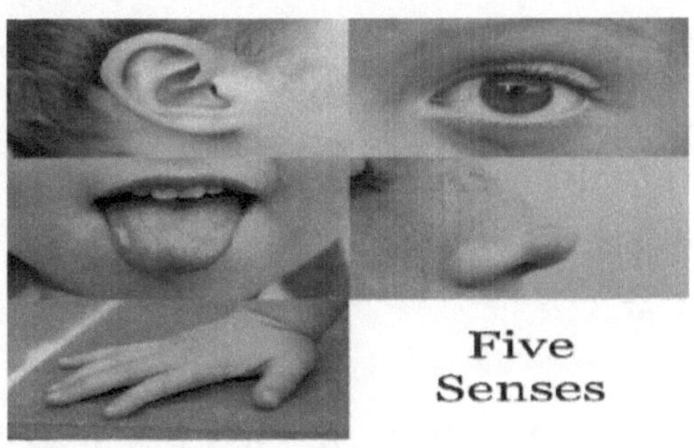



Seeing others in uneasy situations, I am empathetic to their plight. I also know they are at the edge of greatness. Most learning comes with challenges, just as when a meal is cooked there is heat. The heat is energy. We feel the heat and when we learn to use it for the betterment of the meal, we are empowered with wisdom. To sense the heat is the same as to sense love, that feeling of joy or comfort that sends off signals through our bodies and we say, "I feel love."

The requirements to have love feelings are based on each individual's perspective. Many make it almost impossible to receive these love feelings.

**Why not make it easy to feel love, so everything would help you feel love throughout your day?**

After I started to ask this of myself, I found love and peace in almost every single person, place and thing. When it appears that love might be hiding, I simply change my perspective and rise up to discover where that love is.

In many people, love is hidden by anger, which is only a form of fear.  Love could be hidden by greed, another form of fear.

Fear of losing out is another.  Love lies hidden behind mistrust, another fear tactic of losing out.

It looks like a pattern might be appearing.

Love and peace are on one side of joy and happiness. Fear, loss and anger are on the other side.

Could it be that simple? Love or fear, good or bad, her or him, hot or cold, in or out, right or wrong?  Without up, there is no down.

**What do we do with it, love or fear?**

The big gift given to humanity is free will, the power to truly choose.  We are given the opportunity to interpret and choose what sensory information means. Our gift of choice lets us intuitively look for love, no matter how elusive it

may seem to be—or we can choose to respond in fear.
Now, think of love. Where does it hide? Yes, behind fear.

**If we change the way we see fear, we can simply find love in all situations.**

Less-than-positive emotions like fear, hate, greed and anger cover the loss of love. These simple concepts make up the basis of our survival system, and they have been doing their job to get us to this point in our lives. They work very well, but when trauma enters into the system, it can disrupt the balance within the system.

The correction of an unbalanced system is usually some simple method of changing positions, like on a small boat when it is listing to one side, you reposition the person sitting on the side to the middle, which might be only a few inches but the boat is then balanced.

The same applies to feelings. If you are feeling/experiencing a less-than-positive state like fear, you instinctively move away.

What if the pain comes from a spouse?
What if the pain comes from a parent?
What if the pain comes from a co-worker?
What if it is an in-law?
What if it is your child?

**Change the way you perceive them, and you'll gain a new perspective on why love stays hidden.**

How can we change the way we see someone that is so close to us when we already have a strong image of them embedded in our mind?

*Loony Cartoon Reframing a Foe*

With this fun technique I find a cartoon character that best matches the person who is creating fear for me in my experience. In most cases, a cartoon character is much less threatening and enables me to understand them from a totally different perspective. Almost every character has an exaggerated part of their personality that drives them to do some silly things.

The things this person obsesses over simply come from a place of fear. They are attempting to calm fear by inappropriate behavior. When I change the way I see them, I am now empowered to have compassion for their fear state.

I had a boss who was not big on planning and not too organized. He would roll into the room spouting off obscenities and wanting everyone to "jump to it" at his command, which usually had little to do with long-term goals. This was frustrating to me. Then, a character came to me. It was Yosemite Sam. After that, when the boss came in with guns a'blazing, I would simply smile. When his short outburst was over, he was usually out and onto some other "bright shiny object" that caught his eye.

### *Reframing a Foe Process*

Take a moment and think about this. Who in your world gets under your skin? Who rattles your cage and steals your joy? Go back to the time it happened, and picture the scene as though you are a third person viewing from a corner of the ceiling, looking down over what happened.

Now, change the other person into the perfect cartoon character that truly makes you smile. The idea is to transform the situation to be more light hearted and less threatening or stressful. The character can be anything or anyone that helps you feel safer and empowered. You can even change what the person says or does, like from being mean to showering you with flowers.

When you have rewritten your story to your standards and your benefit, simply replay the scene multiple times noticing the shift from negative to positive.

Do you feel a little more at ease this time? Can you laugh inside, knowing how silly they are, for example, throwing a fit like a big baby? Can you see the giant pacifier and the diaper? Or maybe you can imagine them as a tiny little bug and yourself looking down on them with compassion for how petty their tantrum looks from your bigger broader perspective?

With this creative technique, you have the power to reframe any situation to your benefit and your standards from this point forward. Have some fun with it, and intuitively make it part of your daily walk, starting now.

**REFLECTION**

1. Simply make a list of people in your life and their funny cartoon character counterpart.
2. Look back at some of the challenging situations from a third party perspective, like watching on a TV or movie theater.
3. Rewrite the stories that held you back, now focusing on the lessons and how they help you to become stronger.

### *Judging From Love*

*When we fail to see the beauty in others or ourselves it
is due to the filters of fear that blind us
For some reason we have used them to protect ourselves in the past and being creatures of habit we fall
back to what is familiar
So next time you choose to check yourself out in the mir-
ror or have a thought to judge someone or something,
simply stop, close your eyes and take a deep breath
Breathing in all the goodness you can imagine in your
heart, you intuitively scan yourself for the compassion
and love we instinctively have for all things
You can now start to see things through eyes of love
and the perfection of the journey
Easily finding love and caring for ourselves and others,
understanding that without rain, sunny days lose some
of their wonderfulness. When we simply feel love in
ourselves it truly radiates to every aspect of our lives!*

*Tim Skiba*

# Chapter 7

# **Thinking or Remembering**

*Yourself is created by your memories, and your memories are created by your mental habits.*

-Rick Warren

I ask many people if they think more or remember more. What would you say?

As you consider this question for a moment, you might go back to your memories and search for whether you have ever been asked this question. You might even think you should double check your memories, so you can feel good about your answer, probably because when you answer questions correctly it makes you feel good. You can also remember how it feels to be wrong.

In these couple of moments, were you thinking or re-membering?

**"Neuroscientist, Michael Gazzaniga, estimates that as much as 98 percent or more of all brain activity is completely unconscious", leaving only 2% for truly thinking.**

Makes you want to think a little more, maybe?

If we are truly spending most of our time remembering, we must have a pretty sophisticated memory system. Of course, we do. We can mentally return to a place we have only visited once and remember the color of the curtains or the secret trail through the woods or a school locker number and maybe even the combination.

We have a supercomputer in use 24/7. Most of the time, we are simply filing events away and then recalling them later. Some recalls are triggered by similar events, while others are random memories constantly playing in the background. Most of the time, we are only re-membering, not thinking.

Let's test some of this memory stuff since it consumes most of our lives and truly affects the way we interpret every event we experience. Before we test the system, we need to look a little further at judging.

As I mentioned before, judging gets a bad reputation because of political correctness, but it is a necessity for survival. We all do it every day to stay safe. When you understand that you are judging out of instinct, you can become aware of it and start to think, not merely remember.

**Judging is what we do automatically, but how we express this judgment toward ourselves and others is critically important.**

Back to testing our memory system. This is not a test for correctness, but of ways that we organize our memories.

If my question doesn't apply to you, pick a subject of similar content. After a few of these, you will understand and start to realize that although your memory system is unique to you, it operates the same for most everyone.

Our memory system is on all the time, continuously recording and playing back. I call it our holographic memory system. I didn't come up with that name, but it is appropriate to describe how we organize our memories.

**By understanding our memory system, we are empowered to reorganize our memories to benefit our lives.**

This is similar to the way computers have developed. Computers are memory storage systems. Think of the desktop icons or tiles that represent the applications on your phone. Where did the idea of organizing come from as electronic devices evolved? From our own operating system.

No two people could possibly have all the same experiences and, therefore, would not organize their memories the same way. However, many people have computers, and they all work on a binary system of ones and zeros.

**The real difference is how each person organizes their desktop.**

Some might have all the personal stuff to the right or even in the background. Others could have business stuff at the top of their list. The same is true for our own holographic system.

## HOLOGRAPHIC MEMORY TEST

Now, let's run a little test.

If you close your eyes and think of your first day of school, you have a picture associated with it. Where would this picture be in the space around you? In your mind? In your body? In the air in front of you? In back of you?

What about a picture you associate with your first romantic kiss? Is this memory stored in the same place or somewhere else? How about your favorite food? Do you have an image flashing up and a feeling associated with the picture?

We all have similar pictures and feelings connected to them. Where I store my pictures will be different from yours because even though the systems basically work the same, they are all specific to each individual.

Using the information about how we organize our memories, let's play a game with the system. Let's add more good feelings, and, maybe, if you're ready, let go of some less-than-positive ones that might be holding you back.

## Spinning Technique

This technique can be used to intensify positive feelings or to easily transform a less-than-positive state.
Like the exercise before, while working with images
and the feelings associated with them, in and around
your body, you can make positive changes freeing
you from stress and painful memories. Your ability
to be creative in how much energy you expel while
you spin out the negative can be helpful.

Throughout the exercise focus intensely on the color
inside your body, noticing the changes and how easily you can shift things around for your good. Using
this technique is very powerful on all levels of feelings because of how it engages the past and the present,
memories with feelings and colors but most of all you
can work with body sensations without ever seeking
out the root cause.

*Making your change for you and in you, intuitively
creating your best you.*

*Spinning Technique*

Video available at:  https://youtu.be/ikTu57jYqeI

*Warning:  This is a meditative process and you should be in a safe place without interruption and not be driving or operating any forms of equipment. It is recommended that you refer to the audio version and use headphones for best results.*

For positive feelings:

To increase a positive feeling, simply close your eyes and focus on the positive feelings. Picture an image in front of you.

Reaching out and touching the image with your dominant hand and then with your other hand, locating where it is in your body.

See and feel the truly wonderful sensations in your body and touch them.

Looking deep at the sensations with your inner eyes, instantly noticing a color associated with it, your first impression. Black and white are also colors.

Using both hands, reaching in and pulling all that wonderful color, keep going until you easily get it all.

Hold it in your hands.

Notice that it is turning in a certain direction.

Make it spin faster and faster by moving your hands. Double it. Double it again. Focusing on it, spinning it ten times faster and again ten times even faster.

When you have it spinning faster than it has ever been before, according to your standard, and when you are ready, slam it back into your body.

Notice the change. Take a deep breath and simply enjoy the sensations. Whenever you want more positive sensations, simply rinse and repeat!

For less-than-positive feelings:

To dissolve a less-than-positive feeling or physical pain, simply close your eyes and focus on the feeling. Picture an image in front of you.

Reach out and touch the image with your dominant hand and then with your other hand, locating where it is in your body.

Looking deeply at the sensations with your inner eyes, instantly noticing a color associated with it, your first impression. Black and white are colors.

Using both hands, reach in and pull out that color. As you pull it out notice if the color changes or stays the same. Keep going until you easily get it all.

Hold it in your hands.

Notice that it is turning in a certain direction.

Flip it around so it's spinning in the opposite direction.

Make it spin backwards faster and faster by moving your hands. Double it. Double it again. Focusing on it, spinning it ten times faster and again ten times even faster.

When you have it spinning faster than it has ever been before, according to your standard, and when you are ready, slam it back into the same place in your body.

Notice the change. Take a deep breath. Feel the relief.

This can be repeated three or more times if needed to get it all.


**REFLECTION**

1. Make a list of positive memories that you would like to enhance
2. Make a list of less than positive memories that you would like to transform and change your emotional state
3. Throughout your day, ask yourself, are you thinking or remembering

### *Daily Walk*

*You are truly ready to hear and understand the mean-
ing of these words.  We are all given the choice to seek
what we most desire.*

*Most of the time we are merely remembering and moving
towards the familiar, not because it is guiding us to our
best life, but simply because we know what it feels like,
You are worthy to walk along the path less traveled to
find what brings you peace, even if it feels unfamiliar
to you, simply search for the things that bring you joy
and make it your daily walk.*

Tim Skiba

# Chapter 8

# Fear of Worthiness: Living Outside Your Comfort Zone

*Your worthiness is a myth a myth based on your past experience you can boost your self worth by transforming your past*

*By K. N. Pavani*

In my travels and experiences I have met many intelligent, successful people, both male and female and have been surprised by how many of them have struggles with worthiness, despite their many accomplishments, myself included. What does it mean to be worthy? According to the dictionary, the definition is "the quality of being good enough; the quality of deserving attention or respect."

Small shifts in our thinking or beliefs can make monumental changes in our lives. While working with many of my clients I have discovered a language pattern that unknowingly expresses their beliefs.  One such area is the belief of being worthy or not worthy. Clients that believe that they are not worthy use words or phrases like:

I can't do that.

I don't think I could get that house, job, car, friends…. No one wants to listen to my story.

These statements also could be associated with victim language. The techniques throughout this handbook are to help you make change.

I have discovered that everything changes no matter what we do. Each day I get older, thankful for the opportunity to learn and grow. I believe in making the best of each day I am gifted with. The best part of my day is when I can help others. This information and the automated tools and techniques allow me to help others make the positive changes 24 hours a day 365 days a year.

**Change saves years of suffering, years and years and years of suffering!**

Less time suffering leaves more time for gaining the important things in our lives. We all have the power to manifest and to simply start living our dreams.

Thoughts, dreams, wishes are internal and can be held or lost in an instant.

1. First step to make something real is to write it down. Document your dreams, desires, wants, goals.

Then share it with someone, anyone, because when you simply write it down and passionately share your thoughts or dreams with others it opens the doors to the universe to start the process of aligning whatever may need to happen to make it so.

2. The next step should be a plan of action. Steps no matter how few or many, simply start with even the smallest doable step.

Many people journal their thoughts and that is a fantastic way to save and collect your thoughts, but then you must move from passive documentation to share your desires with the universe.

As you start moving through this transformation, your true expectations will be revealed.   Therefore, being clear is extremely important.   The desires that you project out to the universe is what you will get back.

Despite uncertainties and unknowns if you have clear desires and intentions your internal GPS will make the proper corrections to direct you in the right way.

3. Acknowledge to yourself your worthiness to receive your dreams and desires and then open yourself to all the positive energy that surrounds you.


**REFLECTION**

1. Have you done the work?  Ready to receive the rewards?
2. Who do you know that is ready to make positive changes in their beliefs?
3. Do you know who to contact for help in your journey?

Closing Note:

The road was challenging and you looked at some awful situations straight in the eye. When you look at the lessons you have learned and now knowing that you have survived it all, you can easily believe you are truly a **Warrior!**

Yes you may have some wounds and scars but you are a survivor and your knowledge and wisdom from all you have overcome has given you a new perspective, a new strength and a true power, held tightly in your heart.

**Have compassion for yourself first, forgive yourself first.**

Now notice how you are truly different in so many ways. You are different than you were. You are empowered to never look at the past in the same way again. Lay it out in a new way for yourself, and a better way for yourself, which in turn will improve all your relationships.

All your new adventures and challenges simply start with your thoughts of positive possibilities.

Each moment that darkness tries to creep in, your warrior instantly, instinctively appears to guide you through to your new better life to your standards.

If you would like to experience any of the techniques I've shared so far, I'm happy to facilitate the conversation and experience by phone or videoconference.

Simply reserve a time, at your convenience, by going to *www.mindmechanicmethod.com.*

Here you will see an opportunity to get clear on what you want with the 5 Day Shift Your Mindset Challenge or book your appointment for a  session with me to further explore these techniques.

*All writings by Tim Skiba are from his book "Inspira-tional Healing" available digitally or hard copy at
*www.mindmechanicmethod.com*